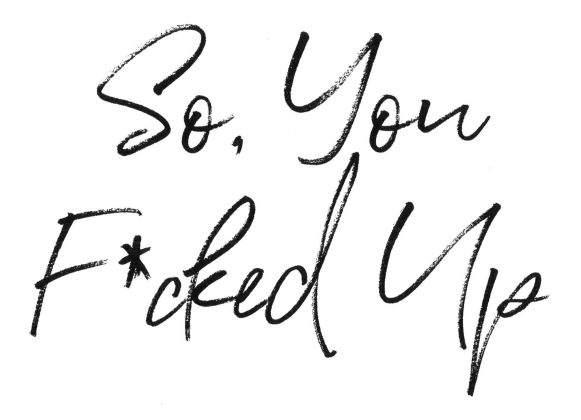

So, You F*cked Up

A Pep Talk for When You've Made a Mistake

MANDI KANE

ARDIA BOOKS

Published by Ardia Books, Nashville, Tennessee

For permission requests, write to the author, at: mandi@mandikane.com

Hardback ISBN: 978-0-578-90196-1

For Sarah.

So, you fucked up.

It's okay.

It happens.

Please don't beat yourself up.

Maybe it was a ᴛɪɴʏ mistake that you can't shake. Maybe it was something **really serious** and you really grilled the cheese. In either case, I suspect you feel pretty shitty right now.

Maybe you feel embarrassed – like you should have known better. Maybe you feel disappointed, because you expected more of yourself. Maybe you're mad. Maybe you're frustrated because you don't have any excuse.

That's okay, no one wants to

hear them anyway.

The truth is, we all make mistakes.

They happen to the best of us,

every day.

You're not alone.

IF YOU'VE MADE A MISTAKE, HERE'S WHAT YOU NEED TO KNOW:

Mistakes are inevitable. No one arrives in this life having everything figured out. Mistakes mean you're trying. Most people spend their whole lives playing it safe. Most people never take a chance.

You are not broken

Those things you tell yourself at night –

the lies that have you tossing and

turning as you struggle to fall asleep –

are not true.

You are not defined by your mistakes,

no matter how public.

BE KIND TO YOURSELF AND BE COMPASSIONATE.

You are a human being
and you are worthy of love,
even on the days when
you haven't done your best.

Own your
behavior.

Apologize if you need to
and be sincere. Saying you're sorry
isn't a weakness, it's a strength.

Find the courage to learn from this.
Lean into the experience and don't
be afraid to ask yourself the tough
questions. More importantly, don't be
afraid of the answers.

You'll do better next time.

You cannot have success
without taking a risk.

Risk makes mistakes possible.

You are fierce.

You are resilient.

You are a
warrior.

So you fell. You can get back up.

You can keep going.

YOU WERE MADE TO WITHSTAND YOUR BAD DECISIONS,

YOUR CHOICES, YOUR MISTAKES.

You
are not

a mistake.

Maybe you did the best you could with what you knew at the time.

You are growing, you are evolving.

You are a different person

than who you were yesterday.

That's a good thing.

This is not a regression.

It's a deviation.

Maybe you need to accept
some consequences.
That's hard, and uncomfortable.
But your story doesn't end here.

Maybe this is where it starts.

Maybe you'll make the same

mistake again at some point.

Maybe you never will.

But you will make another mistake.

And when you do...

YOU'RE GOING TO BE JUST FINE.

Forgive yourself, or at least start the process so others can forgive you too.

You get to choose right now – in this moment – that you are going to let this experience make you better.

How can you learn from this?

YOU'VE SURVIVED EVERY MISTAKE YOU'VE MADE UP UNTIL THIS POINT.

So take a bath.

Make some tea.

Let it go.

Go to sleep because tomorrow,

. you get a fresh start.

You get to start all over.